QUARRY

Quarry: The Collected Poems of Peter Kilgore

North Country Press

NORTH COUNTRY PRESS, UNITY, MAINE

Peter Thomas Kilgore (1941-1992)

Quarry: The Collected Poems by Peter Kilgore

Published 2019 by:

North Country Press

126 Main St.

Unity, ME 04988

www. northcountrypress.com

A number of these poems have appeared in the following publications: *The Cafe Review, Cat Mousam Journal, Contraband Magazine, The Gulf of Maine Reader, Jeopardy, Mom's Apple Journal, Poems on Postcards, Presumpscot Review,* and *Puckerbrush Review.*

Frontispiece and back cover photographs by Carol Kilgore.

Front cover image: detail from 1893 U. S. Geological Survey map of Casco Bay, Maine.

Book design by Michael Alpert.

LCCN: 2019934132

ISBN: 978-1-943424-46-7

for Carol and the kids

Contents

Introduction

Peter Kilgore is a poet of moments, intricate, richly colored occasions, typically physical in focus, engaged ear and eye. Such moments occur everywhere, but for Peter the most vivid occur in the countryside, on the Allagash River in Maine, for instance, or in Casco Bay, off the coast of Portland. These precipitant, often playful times brought forward an element inside of him from which Peter would learn, specifically, how to inhabit experience, in order to align with that external event. That is, his time spent outdoors invoked instances of — Peter's word for this was as a "catalyst" for — engaging in or belonging to that unique moment that each of us is. He wrote from both inside and out — the immediacy, but also the intimacy — of that richness. His poems reflect, then, a preoccupation with the outside as an occasion, but in the full sense of an occasion as being opportune or fit. This collection of his poetry spells that passion out in varied ways, paths Peter took to arrive at and inhabit this place we find ourselves within.

Peter was born on July 28, 1941 to Mervin and Virginia (Abbott) Kilgore and grew up with his brothers Mervin Jr. (Butch) and Michael and sister Nancy on Wilmot Street in Portland, Maine, on the west side, "Bayside," of the peninsula. Mervin Kilgore worked at Randall and McAllister as an oil burner technician and on summer nights, after work and school, father and son played baseball for the Yarmouth Townies in the Twilight Baseball League. Peter took pride in his athletic skills, and as well played baseball and basketball in high school and college. The physical nature of much of his poetry, emphasis on ear and eye, on action (rather than ideas about acting), builds from his athletic experience. But this quintessentially New England neighborhood also became part of Peter's sensibility — he referred to it as his Bayside "work ethic" — and he and friend Bob Armstrong later delighted in recounting episodes from childhood, for Bayside was a palpable cultural location for them. Unfortunately, the neighborhood was demolished in the 1960s for the construction of Kennedy Park and Franklin Street Arterial — "urban renewal" — linking the new I-295 spur to the city's Old Port area. Peter depicts the upheaval in "Portland Renewal Authority."

The Kilgore family owned a cottage on the west end of Long Island in Casco Bay, inherited through his mother's family, the Abbotts, which was a special place for them all. For Peter, time spent on Long Island bordered on spiritual, whether it involved tracking an island fox or watching cormorants wing seaward across Jerry's Point, for island time was a moment in itself. His sister Nancy recalls that as children they experienced an unparalleled freedom to explore and play with cousins and others, one not available to many off-island children. "And if your parents didn't know quite where you were," she comments, "you were under the watchful eye of someone else's parents." In summer, the kids would gather at Southside or Singing Sands Beach, "across the nubble." Their adventures included blueberries, baseball, clamming, climbing about a WWII observation tower, swimming (jumping off the wharf), Wednesday night dances at the VFW hall, and just hanging out "Down Front" — where the ferry docked — for ice cream and dancing to the juke box at the Spar, a small store with benches and an array of penny candy, as well as the scene for summer teen romances. The island was above all their community, their *place* as Peter would have it.

Peter graduated from Portland High in 1959 and attended Bowdoin College, where he first learned of the Beat poets, he said, from William Cohen, the future Maine Senator and Secretary of Defense, Peter's fraternity brother at Psi Upsilon. The Beats, especially the work of Jack Kerouac (another writer with a pronounced New England sensibility), were his lifelong inspiration, as was the poetry of Charles Olson, a poet who distinguished sharply "between language as the act of the instant and language as the act of thought about the instant," the first bearing in on experience, the second away. (Peter quotes from Olson's "The Distances" in his own "Island Poems.") Peter graduated from Bowdoin in 1963 and married Jeanette DiFilippo that year. The new couple moved to Ridgefield, Connecticut, and Peter taught at Wilton High, in the next town over. Peter and Jeanette had two sons, Christian and Kevin. At Wilton High, he met Guy Whitten who invited him to help guide a boys' camp expedition each summer through the Allagash River waterway and down the St. John River to the Atlantic. Peter consequently became licensed as a Maine Guide.

The family returned to Portland in 1970, and Peter went on to teach in the Special Education Department in the Portland school system for

17 years. But Peter had also been writing poetry and in 1971, he approached poet Ted Enslin, living in Temple, Maine, with the manuscript of his first book of poetry, *Openings*, based on that yearly trip to the Allagash. Ted directed him to Bruce Holsapple and Michael Barriault, who had started a small literary magazine, *Contraband*, in Portland that year. In 1972 Contraband Press produced *Openings* in an edition of 300 copies, with illustrations by Portland artist Michael Waterman. When Barriault left the magazine, Holsapple recruited Peter and novelist David Empfield to join him in co-editing nine further issues of the magazine and twelve more chapbooks, including two letterpress editions of Peter's finest work, *River/Road* and *Drinking Wine Out of the Wind*.

These two books are characteristic, but everything about Peter's work — from line lengths and rhythmic structures to imagery — tends to be extremely spare and intricately handled to the point of a tautness. At the same time, he assembled these lines, stanzas and sensibilities into long sequences, from "Allagash" to *The Bar Harbor Suite* (Blackberry, 1987) to "Yellow Aster Butte," that are part narrative and part lyric. Peter carried notebooks on his travels, then transferred his notes onto big sketch pads, the poems spread over two large sheets — 12 by 36 inches — on which he revised them into books, spatially as well as sequentially, so that the poems are textured, woven together. His characteristic spareness is evident throughout his writing, from the early sequence "3 POEMS for jack kerouac," which provides sharp, evocative biographical sketches of Kerouac, all the way to "Descending Down to My Roots" (completed in 1991 and published in *Puckerbrush Review* in 1999) and "Coast to Hope Coast," completed in 1991 but unpublished before now, loosely based on the inner journey of his move from Maine to Washington state. The sonic, visual and tactile imagery crystallizes, in a way parallel to how Sufi poets use the metaphor of drunkenness, into what reads best as a narrative of numinous experience. The sense overall is that a close and unusual, perhaps unique, spirituality pervades our lives and is always at hand.

Peter and Jeanette divorced in 1977. In 1978, Peter married Carol (Hess) Eliot, another summer resident of Long Island, who had known Peter from childhood, and they had two children, Kalen and Shawnee. (Peter's *Elegy* was written for Carol's father, Karl Hess, an inveterate sailor.) The new family relocated from Portland, with Carol's two boys from her previous marriage, Ehben and Trent, to Babbidge Road in West Falmouth, where they restored an older farmhouse. In 1987, they sold that house and moved again, this time to Sumas, Washington, where Peter worked in the local library while restoring another old house. He continued to write and publish in Maine periodicals, and he revisited the state in 1989, '90 and '91. In the winter of 1991-92, Peter sought psychiatric help in Washington state for severe depression. He was prescribed Prozac, a controversial drug, at least at the time. He took his life on February 4, 1992.

Some 25 years later, he continues to be missed, but the poetry speaks as richly as ever, and it's that intricately measured voice we would call attention to, for its resonance and for its play, its way of speaking to, as well as of, his experience. This collection was drawn from all known published works, as well as several manuscripts Peter had circulated among friends, with three exceptions. The manuscripts of "Island Poems," "Yellow Aster Butte" and "harbor songs" were culled from hand-written worksheets, although Peter had published poems from those manuscripts individually. We should also add that our section, "Poems in Manuscript," is arranged in roughly chronological order from the 1970s to the 1990s.

– Bruce Holsapple
Dana Wilde
Fall 2017

QUARRY

Openings

for jeanette and guy

Let the unspoken words
be unthought for the pen
inscribed for the intended
to know and care
that I was there.

I asked him, What do you do?

*He smiled patiently. The typical American question.
In Europe they would ask, What are you doing? Or,
What are you doing now?*

*What do I do? I listen, to the water falling. (No
sound of it here but with the wind!) This is my entire
occupation.*

–William Carlos Williams, *Paterson*

I Penobscot

i
Speed
over blacktop
from the symmetry
of cities
to lonely roads
out of the way
walk dirt trails
to the waterway
enter a different
wilderness.

Like a sea-run salmon
I have returned
to a darkened crib
by an inland sea
where man beheld
the mystery of growth
and fled afraid.

I feel again
the rhythms of sun
sowing the constant
seeds of survival
from a day
in the season
to a cycle of years.

Regain a world
where the clock
is not
minute enough
nor great enough
to govern life
but where
there is time
time enough
to know
the slow
unfolding
of a flower.

ii
return
no fear
no urgency
only to be

standing in
the forest again

after a long
penitential year

iii
I lie
beside the water

where the river

descends
the stairs
in white

silent
on a precipice
wind beckons
descent

iv
Where the stream
enters the river
currents have washed
the earth away.

Trees still grow
from the sunken banks
bending their trunks
above the water.

They might be
the faces of children
leaning over
to look in the sea.

v
Two trunks stand

massive in midstream
hollow gray with
time and weather
crests blackened by
lightning strikes.

Green forests
leave the banks
and the river
without looking
still passes by
the charred remains
leaning together.

vi
In the pool
behind me
lies a doe
belly-up
as pallid as
a dead fish.

Except for the
undevoured flesh
one might think of
bears or bobcats
stalking forest
in pursuit of
existence.

She must have come
to the river
to drink.
Summer had been
hot and dry.

Between the flash
and the impact
she tried to
twist from death.

The unsprung body
shattered the pool
eyes wide
to the waters end.

Her undersides
as she lies there
growing green with mold
are as white as milk
spilled in the grass.

vii
Back from the trout
back from the incessant churning
of brown water over brazen stone
between the alders that crowd the stream
the forest opens to emptiness.
A floor of moss so tender

it could not support the trees
but silenced them in their fall
covered them in their decay.
Now bloom death-born flowers
delicate above the luscious grave.
Summer warriors lie at rest
in a spruce hollow of moss and rust
under a shower of sun fragile rays.

viii
Bed this noon
was bearded rock
where I lay
and watched
clouds pass by
until with stream
and branches of wind
I warmly slept
in sun.

And Jesus—the hawk
so high I
barely realized
he wheeled above
I stared afraid
to let him go
one glide
motionless
across sky

he passed
from my vision
just faded
back to blue.

ix
Small birds
struggle so
to fly
as do
butterflies.

Insects have
their own
dangerous
existence.

But who
can touch
the hawk.
Who can
touch the hawk.

x
The stream is narrow
and tortuous
suggesting a passage
of smoke
on the wind.

In shallows
near the shore
lilies pale
as water mixes
grass and reeds
with the remnants
of trees.

A forest died here
flood inverted
water bound
to drive torn roots
into air
dying unearthed
in twisted despair.

There is quiet
in this wilderness
all that remain
are skulls –
blanched skulls
and broken limbs.

And in the silent
growth of grass
the stream etches
an epitaph.

xi

a tree

wavers in wind

grows green

and sheds

needles to earth

where perfect

cones lie

like mute shells

on ocean shore

tokens of a season

spent to the sun

xii

Toward dusk

a thunderstorm

huge thunderheads

swollen black

with chilling rain

ending in

a double rainbow

arch over arch

over half

the horizon

xiii

Alone among

pine and spruce
an aged birch
spreads white limbs.

xiv
A strong breeze
from the northwest
an orange sun
in a hazy
western sky.
With tolling bell
the logging camp
grants the trees
a night of rest
where a solitary
crow can row
above the dark
horizontal shore.

xv
nightsound

the sharp bark
of an awakened sense
the hungry pack
senses can be

xvi
Weary lids and

long lashes
slowly cover
the evening sky.

I lie alone
beneath the stars
while constant
fingers of wind
awaken my hair.

II   Allagash

i
A blue day
with mounting
white clouds
sky vagrants of
indifferent pace.

But on
the horizon
a band of grays
gallops above
the trees.

Cloud frieze
in sky temple
one line of

contrasting darks
low charging bulls
the spirit of
the buffalo.

ii
Through eons of growth
this island knew
the dry rasp
of chaff on stone
until a wind-blown
piece of sun
stunned the ridges.

As cinder arcs
engraved the air
seed-wings
spiraled to earth
like green feathers
from a hawk-struck bird.

Now finger roots
grasp the stone.
The promise of trees
splits the air
with limbs that pulse
of sapling fire.

iii

The railroad trestle
that spanned the lake
stands like
the charred remains
of timberline.
Uneven pillars
feeble with age
unshoulder their burden.
Rusted track
twisting in space
finally concedes to
the water below.

At the tramway
the remains of a station
where miles of track
traversed the ground
a main cabin
several shacks
and a weathered barn.

But the cabin is broken
the shacks dilapidated
the track overgrown
with alder cover.

Stabled in the barn
the engines retain

something of majesty
two massive black chargers
once the pride
of pulpwood land.
Now blind and
heavily haunched
they bide their time
branded by those
who never knew them.

No proud
black mane
trails the wind
no whitened breath
as they crest hills.
All is gone.
Retired.
An era ended.
Empty hulks
allow inspection.

iv
subdued day
sun-mesmerized
windless lake
lies hypnotized

only hawk
moves on the eye

tracing circles
in sunfaded sky

v
This lake lives
in loneliness
surface seen by some
depth touched by few
vast reservoir surface
ripples with smiles
invites the sun
but few have
plunged so deeply

finger breaks
the surface
touches flesh
to flesh

vi
the hand
of a cloud
closed over
the sun

vii
Earth stands
veiled in mist
with white

upon the water.
Leaves scurry
anticipating rain
as swollen clouds
sweep the sky.
Spirited winds
ride the lake
driving waves to shore.

Almost like
the ocean
it seems.
At times
almost a sea.

viii
Pines roar.
Some say whisper
but only as ocean
whispers from far
closer it's a roar
the roar of
a billion needles
vibrant in breeze
the sound of fire
fed with wind.

ix
across the lake

black with night
cloud fringe
is luminous yet
although the sun
has already set

x
Day had been dry
but during the night
talons of lightning
flashed at earth.
Deep thunder
erupted overhead
rolled mumbling
under the sky
and night awoke to
rain-dark wings.

xi
In semblance to
a sunless dawn
day is long
and gray.
Mist and fog
cloud the shores.
Waters are blown
silver-gray smoke.
Wind increases
mist to rain

waves to shore.
Loons echo
hollow lament.
Time to recede.
Wait.

xii
rainfall

on the far shore
hills and trees dissolve
in a dark confluence
of waves and clouds

xiii
flowers that closed
against the rain
open again

with colors as faint
as the rain scent
of earth

xiv
Wild strawberries
between grass and stone
a solitary iris
wild purple
in reeds

a fallen tree
remembered in moss
in the rain
woven forest.

xv
rain-capped
wildflowers
glisten in
puddles of sun

xvi
seen from a
mountaintop
after a shower

rainbow
arches above
the lake
below

xvii
hazy day
sun wades
through fields
of mist

xviii
red squirrel

scampering
fiendish big-eye
brown in
hue

water lily
golden quiet
serenely anchored
in roughened
lake

wild iris
peppering
driftwood gnarled
and lakeside
green

xix
and I sit
throwing pebbles
into a calm lake

and gaze upon
the silver-beaten
path of sun

xx
waterfall is
sound at first

the distant thunder
of water on stone
closer becomes
the essence of time
elementary change
in a flood of white

xxi
river strength
surges over the
unearthed shoulders
of monoliths who
brace their backs
against the flow

pulses white
among bones
healing the gash
torn centuries ago
when glacial fingers
gouged earth

xxii
pristine beauty
of falling water
shaping stones
with a rainbow torch
drives bluebells
through the rocks

xxiii
sunset

in a golden nest
the firebird folds
his wings to rest

xxiv
Sky above the inlet
is clear and fully pink
fading upward to neutral tones.

Around the lake
mountains of trees
begin to darken
as if green sap
descends with sun.

Terns shriek
over darkening water.
Shapes scamper
before nightfall.

xxv
Dusk envelops a willing lover
easily drawn down and under
yielding to the great serene.

Tall pine against sky

I silently stand
limbs outstretched
to await the night
to await the dawn
and welcome wind and rain.

And in the midst of change
having growth
I change.

xxvi
Of evening
in wilderness
awe and reverence
only.

Unquestioned mystery
spruce vaults
under towering stars
being in beauty
of truth beyond
and not of man.

Feeling within
I do not pretend
to comprehend
the spiritual passage
of strength.

III Saint John : The Run to the Sea

i
among the rocks
along the stream
lie stale shells
that insects shed

transparent overlays
of the living bug

ii
I quiver
in current
like a quick
trout

turn fin
and dart

downstream

iii
A doe and two fawns
arch their necks
to drink from
dull brown pools.

iv
wind

in fields
of grass
beyond
the border

buffalo backs
swell
in sun

v
trees with
branches
spread like
hands

spans of
evergreen
under sky

vi
white pine
with massive limbs
holds fields of green
above the ground

vii
in daytime
over the village
the whiteness of
a quarter moon
waits for night.

viii
I have lain
for days
watching sky
fields of blue
with herds of
wild stallions
cloud-manes
unfolding in wind
wisps winding off
fading like dust
to nothingness.

ix
thoughtless
existence
just being
cloud like
river like
like a tree

x

Air is alive

in a final

surge of green.

Crickets promise

a constant grate

as darkness

descends river.

Grass pumps

as a logging truck

growls through town

strident horn

wounding night.

xi

water

whose youth

is roaring

falls

white

with age

flows

to sea

to merge

endlessly

xii
clouds

on barren beaches
in an icy clime
blond innocents
silhouette
the ice blue snow
where an old man sits
in the emptiness
of afterseason

xiii
And so I return
to the sea again
from transient pine
to constant salt
the sudden peace
of restfulness.

I sit on a bench
fenced from sea
where life
laid over cables
is gone
ocean-cradled.

I have opened

sleep-black eyes
the dark aching
of moments past
awaken in depth
as of the sea
fall under
the mystery
as man to woman
approach the sea.

xiv
children play
sandpiper-agile
on the barefoot beach

xv
A stifled scream
as I pound
down the shore
in an excited
dance to existence
catch salt air
where islands grow
like dark hedges
in a sea of grass.

xvi
arms of white

embrace the cove
as if this were
the edge of existence

xvii
I cross the bridge
at the borderline
find you
close and green
rooted to sea.

When I taste
your salt
I stir
hearing surf
swelling breasts
in endless
ebb and flow
I pierce
pine thighs
lost in landscape
bare to the sky.

Breathing bodies
of heather and moss
I crest into
a flood of salt
and inundate
familiar shores.

Poems in Magazines, 1971 – 1978

§　Elegy

i

She writes
on the calendar
makes it a diary
of the year's events
briefly scratched
in squares of time.

Come November –
clean white sheet –
she inscribed
in the first plot
'Al died.'

ii

Leaving the town
we followed the pavement
through the hills/
clouds of milltown
passed hunters
watching fields
or walking ridges
found Bear River
and around the bend
the homeland.
Newry mountains.
Burial ground
beside the road.

iii

this is the land
of my fathers

where they left
the land
ran to cities
return to land

where his dust ends
mine begins

iv

I remember green —
this country green
of mountain farms
sudden air after
boy-long trips
the weariness
of that travel

trout through fields
behind the house
country stores
abandoned farms
iron and rust
in knee high grass

nights as dark
as a mountain lake
when they talked
and I lay there
in a farm-cold bed
until morning sun
and coffee rays

§   "in town"

in town
old women

whisper in
restaurants

pasted like
leaves

along
the aisles

it is
the dead
of winter

§

She sits in silence
like an unlighted room
overlooking the sea.

Across the bay
the dark depth
of flint mountain
swells in the night
like a clenched fist.

There was a time –
a night of love
when they lay revealed.
Lost warmth and laughter
have hardened them so.

There is no resolve
when she rises for sleep.
Against the blackness of night
she unfolds her days
like fresh white linen.

§

He might always
have belonged to the sea.

Squat like a block
of sea rock
eyes sea-weed brown
when weed is wet
and shines in the sun.
Shells of pearl
break from red
and salt-stained hair.

Amphibious
he comes ashore
occasionally.
More often he
finds his peace
away from men.

He and I
sat by the shore
talking together
where we'd been
what we'd done
since the war
how we fit in
the peace we'd made.
We laughed together.

You sat away from us
away and above
on a large sea rock.
You might have been
on a mountain top
listening to echoes
from valleys below.

And when
we were alone
you said
we shouldn't
have stopped.

§

walking with
my son today
i was like
a grandfather
letting the boy
have his way
drawing me along
on invisible strings
until we came
to railroad tracks
that split the town
like a double seam.

i took the lead
walking the ties
of twenty years –
hoping he followed

§ **wing beats**

for Sherry

you have
touched my
wing

taken my
feathers

wear them
where you

soar

§ **apology for silence**

i have
nothing
to say

this is
a time
of decision

the arguments
presented

a time
of weighing

myself
the jury

or accused

§ **prometheus**

cold
it was
the second
of april

until
i stole
the fire
of your
thighs

god
i was

cold

§

for you
i become
bird

hair feathers
arms wings

cock of eye
i cock

cockwalk
watch

my incred-
ible dance

FFFFURRRRR
FFFFURRRRR

STHURUMMMP
THERUMMMMP

§

How can I say that wind
stirs the water to waves
waves that move against the rocks
move against the shore.

And if I should speak
then to whom
when sun has set
and wind has risen
on an ember evening
and we lie unafraid
beyond time.

§   **for Carroll Tarkarski**

We were working
on the roof
in early spring
when Ski came by.
He had lasted another
winter alone
tweed coat, baseball cap
face chicken thin, stubbled.
We talked from the roof
for a while
until we came down
to be closer.

your eyes relived
mudslide days
bare-ass with girls
ballroom dancing
you learned with your eyes
clubs and floors
Irishmen different
from the Poles

you mimic the native
his arrogance of new job
throwing your jagged
shoulders back
head up, chin out
lips pulled back
like strips of liver

We leave the cold
for coffee in the house
yours light –
watery by choice.
Scratching your head
adjusting your hat
you smoke and talk
with the slight breath left.
Spirit some say.

coronets and violins
sliding leather shoes
meticulous youth
a bastard – your word
canoe rides in the dark
pillows and blankets
bootleg pints
women like the panama canal
go straight in
never touching a side

*"I had lots of friends
on the waterfront.
Fraternity, you know.
Jesus I was strong.
I could one-arm
my fifty-horse."*

When he first came
he frightened us all
a fisherman among
the summer folk.
He took the house
where we took water.
Blocked the paths.
Didn't need us around.
Some sudden phrase like
"How'd you like
kids nosing around
when you're bare-ass
with your wife?"
And he kept those dogs
to keep us away.

We used to watch him
working his boat
while we swam
at the beach.
Passed him on the road
head down in
fisherman's clothes.
Sinews. Shining skin.
An awesome sight
when he was younger
or we were younger.
Even in our safest places
we left you alone.

friend
your face
has lost its edge
as has your voice
you're more frequent now
as if you've held us
on your terms too long
kept more than your bare-ass
years to yourself
in living the sea
you've almost become
an island

§ **mort**

a root
of a man
not the bulk
of oak or elm
but sinews
of alder
green and angled
close to the ground

or a knot
in a place of pine
all the hardness
and dark pitch
twisted into
one tight orb
morning cough
the logger comes

§   **for father Marquis**

friend

you know
seeing you here
in this wilderness

does not disturb
the balance
of things

3 POEMS *for jack kerouac*

§   **town & city**

New England life
close to earth
family proud
labor man
homespun wife
nucleus for children
spinning through seasons
intent to cling
against the spin
whirling cosmos.

From boss to jobber
farm to flat.
Milltown. Open fires.
Dump picking
for auto parts.
Rock fight
jealousies.
Tenement life.
Disintegration.

He tightens. Curses.
Tries to hold.
They strain to gain
spinning further
faster drawn by
spinning force
stretched taut
center snaps
casting orbs
into the void
of wartime America
the great wandering
each attracted
or attracting
seeking orbits
of their own.
Ashes for some.
Others begin again.
Except this one –
a brilliant comet
from coast to coast
and back again
searching for
an elusive center.

§   on the road

America has always been
there for the traveler
from the Aleutian landbridge
to the Atlantic Ocean
rivers and streams
footpaths trails
a network of highways
between the oceans.

Jack on the road
all that traveling
busing hitchhiking
hiballing the raw body
of the country itself
Jack on the road
coming home or leaving
chasing the real
sirens of America.

Jazz. Sweating. Jazz.
night talking jazz

driving jazz

Dean's cars
    across the country
        jazz roads

New York to Denver
    Denver to Frisco
        Frisco New York

New York New Orleans
    Orleans to Frisco
        Frisco New York

New York to Denver
    Denver to Frisco
        Frisco New York

New York west

Mexico City sickness
New York City again

Times Square. Alone.

Broke. Breaking.

Where Dean?
Where everybody?
Where life?

Lonesome traveler
lights are dim
across America.
In my own time
I know of Dean.
Cassady dead
on the railroad tracks.
And Jack dead
deep in the South.

Not yet wholly buried.

Not yet holy.

Buried.

§   **loves of a generation**

           i

New Year's Eve America
Lowell's urchins
walk the streets
on the way to a dance
pushing shoving
impulses of growth
bumping rearing
like ponies
not yet broken

'no idea in '39
that the world
would turn mad'

ii

Maggie Cassidy
high school queen
Marguerite Casa d'Oro
she was fire smoldering
he was only 16
with a Catholic cock

he never did
get in her pants

iii

meanwhile his father
was walking along
the red brick walls
of commercial Lowell
looking for a job
something lost
between the man
and the boy –
father and son
growing up with
women between

iv

Springtime prom
society's youth
in society's tower
powders graces
gowns and laces

waltzing through
the formal daze

Well Maggie –
here it is –
New York

I don't
give a shit
she said
leaving the
stage

v

3 years later
after the dreams
they end up in
a Lowell garage
where he works
– no talk –
he tugging
at her girdle
she laughing
in his face

he never did
get in her pants

§   DRAFTS

it has to do
with light –
the lightness
of this event

an aura of
soft blue

freeze
summerian
frieze
with the
suggestion
of cool —

MOVE

———

there seems
to be only
good here
goodness &
good people

shades of gray
but brightest
light
burning thru

(to you)

———

you hold
his hand
to your
cunt

as if
by fingers
hand & arm

you would

draw him
back

stuff him
into
your dark
hole

forever

smile

———

he lights
his cigarette
with one hand

so well
she says

blue smoke

beats
of music
hearts

sequence
sequitur
sequuntur

teacher
TEACHER

———

she holds
his hand
above her

womb

the mother
of children
misunderstood

the seriousness
of it all
mother & child

i expect
to see a tear

instead

her sudden
laugh

god
i could
embrace you all

i can
embrace

you all
you know

———

me –
i'd rather
be –

with her
over there

at the next

table

touch me
in the

morning

———

english girl
(you seem)

hair skin
bandana

the close
teeth
sweet
red smile

upstairs
downstairs

the back
door

———

tonight

word to
word

glass to
glass

she has
her arm

around me
lip to
lip

later

breast to
breast

& whatta
bust

§   **A Poem of Naming**

Jerry's Point.

That's what I've known
since I walked here as a boy.

The name fit then.
My world was growing with people.

I still take my place here.
But from years of walking and watching
I find the name no longer fits.

I would have it
the Place where Cormorants Cross.

They fly easily through the bay
along the shore close to water.

But here they rise in ancient routes
swing into wind cross the point
wing their way to open sea.

Gulls ride here too
terns dive swoop past
the cormorant

breaking through
or hiballing in
from Outer Green.

§   **donna**

you
in new
orleans

lipton soup
in a 2 room
flat

your winter
coat here

in the north
clean green

shape
taken out
on an iron
hanger

bayou

good bye
you

bayou babe

§ 'Z'

i saw
your father
today

last i knew
he was
hospital-
ized

but today
i saw him

sitting
in a blue robe

smiling
like a buddha

from his city
porch

§   Portland Renewal Authority
Franklin Arterial : Cathedral Square

franklin street: bing chous laundry jacks barber
shop the house where myrna lived diamond meat
market diagonal front cut off the square a single
pillar & thumb latch doors a sawdust store of
mustachioed men in stained white aprons gray men
with red faces reading kitchen notes from women
they knew freezers of beef & pork hung from hooks
meat cut cleavers on butcher blocks behind the
counter white twine clinging from a metal cone

bob macks clothes for men with tinted yellow
plastic behind the glass no room to move no air
to breathe but pile on pile of pants & shirts
aisle on aisle of jackets coats clothes for workers
& service men wearever heavy goods in dark green or
pale blue with company patches & sewing machine
scrawl

lincoln park grocery store paper rack & fruit stand
on the sidewalk dark shadows inside boxes of penny
candy where the cash register was returnable bottles
kept in wooden crates baked goods canned goods pet
food soap metal ice cream case soda case glass &
white dairy case with clasp handles of cold steel
that clicked open chunked shut or up those 3 stairs
to the back room where a spout came through the
wooden floor long crank handle bubbling oil in
glass jugs

quincy street no longer there pelletiers soft
speaking frenchmen row on row of mirrored tonic
water splashed on rubbed in bringing tears to eyes
slicked down drying stiff robe brisked off with
there you go son standing new searching for quarter
coat & out the door

gregesons frosted cakes good luck to make you grow
specials in season from ovens out back hot cross
buns with red & green spices raisins inside stand
& wait try to decide for patient ladies in powder
& rouge

hansens drug store cures in small green bottles
hollow clunk on empty glass on marble top jesus
never fails first baptist 5 & 10 K of C multi-
colored pittsburg paints army navy tenement houses

of myrtle & stone abandoned runs up & down the
marble steps of city hall around the plaza through
iron gates lobsterman pause lobsterman run coat
free laughing feet splatting through & out the
door to woolsen school & cumberland avenue boys
club or to the lunch stand in the pearl street
post office where the blind man sold & counted
change

past insurance company gilded gold chamber of
commerce stone church of sunday life apartment
buildings with wooden doors & fancy names elm
street bowling alleys & roller rink or
museum quiet against noise & motion edwards &
walker hardware store playland lined with pinball
machines deft nudge flip sharp crack of free game
royal flush speedway thrills to preble street
portland theater 10 cent saturday features no
plush red quiet of state or strand but screams
of horror joy & play echoed from balcony to
bottom floor johnny mac brown whip wilson lash
larue ending in lights after 2 times through
blinking into the dim outdoors

today I walk & see:

TURNER BARKER BUILDING
WINTER SALE
QUODDY MOCCASINS
SUPER SOLES SUPER SOLES

OPEN TILL 9
I'M OK YOU'RE OK
SEAGULL FINE
THINGS FOR PETS

WATER AT YOUR SERVICE
WINTER WHITE SALE
CHARGE IT
INTEREST FREE

DO YOU HAVE A
CHARGE ACCOUNT
BONDED & INSURED
OPENING SOON

IF YOU DON'T START
  SAVING NOW
WILL YOU EVER START
  SADDLE UP & GO

GET HONEST
  TASTE
BETTER DEALS
  BETTER SERVICE

NO IFS
  NO ANDS
    NO BUTS

YOU MUST BE
  SATISFIED
WITH EVERY PURCHASE

River/Road

for Norma

§

tedium of lights
GREEN GREEN

i have been
city too long

fields too long
village forest

TOO LONG
TOO LONG

§

tension of
fog dusk travel
driving truck
through
strains of smoke
strains of talk

until we reach
BACKROADS
lakeside friendship
cedar smell

§

the weight of ax
unsheathed

wait of hands on
handle again

sounds & feel
of splitting wood

EMBERS
in night air

SMOKE THOUGHT
FIRE

§

SLEEP

SLEEP   WIND

SLEEP   RAIN

SLEEP

BIRD SONG

SUN

§

WALKING
below the falls

i saw trees
mounting trunks
straddling stone

A STUMP

as hollow
as a 3 foot
plant pot

& i know
if i look inside

JESUS – YES
2 SEEDLINGS

growing glowing
in the dark rot

§

SO SMOOTH

my canoe
& i

a dragon-
fly

rides us

for miles

§

SUN CLOUDS
mid-morning

just poled
& pulled
3 miles

upstream

he calls me

to portage
canoes
around
the dam

but these
BERRIES

are so
GOOD

§

for the one
who left
a bouquet

of daisies
violets &
hawkweed

hanging limp
from the ridge-
pole

i had been
paddling
all day in rain

they warmed me

more than tea

they warmed me

§

SITTING ON
BOULDERS

just above the
tops of cedars
that rise from
lakeside below

looking down
thinking
of han-shan

when a black
& white moth
lights on my arm
gives me a feel

WAY UP HERE

§

WEARY
COMING DOWN

the trail
to allagash
mountain

i rose to
wildflowers

tucked in
red hair

wanetta   i knew
i would find you

WILD

this summer

§

Old Mert
has a new
woman
they say

he may be
leaving
after all
these years

say she's
pulling him
closer to
farmington

every day
they say

§

ANDROSCOGGIN
RIVER

the sign said

i looked
out window
to highway
below

cold & gray

RIVER / ROAD

Drinking Wine Out of the Wind

for J

§

In Portland Harbor

THERESA
CARACARA
APRIL GALE

LADY OF
     THE GULF

SKIPJACK
SAINT JUDE

§

i can't
remember
her name

lisa / laura

until I
imagine
greeting
her again

How are
you –
JU –
     LIE
(YES)

& now
leaving
portland

it seems
(JULIE)
too ornate

§

my friend
on this island
has diabetes

or

it's when your
fecal matter …
your bowel stuff

DAMa-
riscotta

Nice aw-
ful Nice

old lady
sneeze

§

you sure
of this ?

i've seen
it happen so
many times

after he

came back

he had this
devilish smirk
on his face

he roamed
& he wandered
he wandered
& he roamed

what he needs
is a good
sound thrashing

§

1 silhouette
running up
the wharf

2 silhouettes
onto land

BARNACLE
PILES BUN-
YON CAR-
BUNCLES

rain-slick
cliffs

this depth
of green

§

cormorant
song

shag
black

head &
neck

ass —
as he

dives

§

i'm
for
joy

for
spon-
tane-
ity

(trance
opens

to her
stare)

§

Hussy. Sound.
Growl. Honey

a toy poodle
black with
rhinestones
& a red leash

would you like
some honey
on your toast

honey in your tea

sea breeze

§

now this a-
mazes me

& I let
him have it

right in
the ear

§

in a
rock
garden

just off
the road

CRO
CUS
ES

year's
first

flow-
ers

§

SMOKE
low in fog
& rain

driftwood
on the roof

country music
(Michael)

inside

§

from Fowler's
Beach

2 sand
dollars

&

a piece
of blue

glass

§

Billows. Buffeting.
No balance for birds.
WINDSTUNNED

tossed a-
cross sky

or driving
low & slow
into wind

just above
the waves

§

O-
CEAN

send
me

your
biggest
wave

(all
clichés)

YOUR
AWE

§

3 blue
herons

sideways
wingflap
fall

SOCKO
(SIROCCO)

slammed
in the face

by fists
of warm
wind

§

camel
clouds
race

halfway
down
below
the belt

black
humps of
cloud

leave
the sun

§

SCUD

jesus h
CHRIST
what a day

catches
in my craw

day ? late
afternoon

but sun
has just

BROKEN
THROUGH

a powder haze

of cloud & fog

§

GULLS
at dusk

LOOM

(materialize)

pinions
knit in

a ridge
of wind

§

early morning
sun on sand

micascopic
universe
PING

i will
what i will

MASTER
PIECES

splash
my world

images swirl

CALLIOPE
BRAIN

§

AMBERGRIS

every
fashionable
lady's wish

kelp/dulse

ANGELHAIR

there's flies
in the sea
weed

§

walking the backroads
from the morning boat
thinking about spending
a day at the quarry

watching for hawks –

like this one here
leading me on
in a high glide
straight to the point

§

Gale Winds
take it
from the top

peel back
teeter tack

Great Black
Backed Gull

BREAKING
THROUGH

§

i high
on grass

see
  eider
    down

the
  outer
    side of

Overset

§

seeing
sparrow

dart from
bush

i crouch

*   *   *

BRANCHES
talk
to me

§

WINO
OF THE
WORLD

huddled in a
harbor of stone

drinking wine
out of the wind

stunned by flap
above & behind

6 cormorants
in wind

low (THEIR
EYES) shift

from me

§   A CROWBOY'S JOY

     I walk Big Beach to the point. Wince when sun sinks behind clouds. It's too cold here to wait for sunset. I cross Fowler's hunched. Eyes on rimes of sand small dunes catching western sun. Billygoat the path in front of Bean's cross the strip to Mt. Hunger but cut away from the usual path.

Instead I head for the rocks where Bill Floyd used to moor his boat. Push thru scrub brush and sumac to a patch of grass high above the water. I stand on flat top boulder chunks mocking crows awkward in wind. Stumble caw a dozen more confused at my call circle back tack inland one over the flock around.

I backtrack toward the quarry where they blasted breakwater stone for Overset. A small crescent of juniper and willow. Rough rockslide sides. I like to lie inside the western cusp watching sea birds ride the winds. I draw strength here I have power.

Still laughing with crows I crest the northwest rim stop to gawk as two hawks shot from rocks like puffs of dust in this gale wind. My power! My joy! My place on earth!

§

Open
to ex-
panse

expend-
able
spend-
thrift

spin
drift
&
wind
fall

golden
apple

of the
sun

§

this day's
wine
is mine

rake of wind

earaches
of wind

rapier wind

i'll be
this day's
monk

Island Poems

§

winter consortium
sentinel
cardinals
jay squawk
chickadee
the wind high
in trees
velvet spikes
of staghorn
sumac
soft fur
against
the snow
fruit on pale limbs
wine cups
uplifted
apple scrolls
the noon sky
bows of waves
soft breasts
of tide lips
of foam

§

Michael up
early this
morning
practical
walking
the boundary
looking for
blow down
after last

night's storm
firewood
for winter
2 small
oak & an
elm

§

like deer
or moose
i amble

any tract
will do

day calls
& i move

the only
tracks
are mine

§

in the
bay

the bare
spines

of winter
islands

bare limbs
under
white dust

this is
the paring
down

cold bone
under
taut skin

facets
of a
winter
wave

§

winter beach
ocean & ice

in the sand
a single shell

BLUE HORSE
MUSSEL

an empty
heart

hinged open

§

strong brine
scent of
fresh sea-
weed

lodges in
the back
of my throat

dulse
ripening
in the sun

whole trees
of it
torn up

§

walking chilled
looking out
across the sound
the fractured liquid
of winter sea
another flock
low coming from
behind College Rock
black shags in
a gallery row
each zen
moves the others
i cannot stay them
from their course
stop & watch them

cross Hussey Sound
turn my back
as they pass the point
hollow thunder
resounding from Overset
above the decoys
in december air
sun as cold
as an eider's eye

§

that sound
again

breakers
crush
the cove

surge, the
suck & draw

the hollow
clatter

of small
rocks

caught
in the wave's
rake

§

big loon

alone in
the cove

bobs / dunks
his head
among
lobster
traps

rides with
wind &
currents
on the
wave

gone

§

crows in
heavy wind

it's almost
as if they
don't know
what they're
doing

long chains
of crow
buffeted
black powder
away in wind

at times they
almost collapse

with effort
give in

yet gather
& then

§

& still i
marvel at them

pick them up
rub their beauty
with my thumb

these brilliant
little stones

wet in the sand
bright in the sun

how they fade
eclipsed in pockets

as keepsakes
taken home

§

the hollow
stalks of yarrow
seer arms
with dry
joints
fingers

cupped
up to sun
palms
full of seeds

§

leaving
i have
arrived

§

wind in
the dunes

the bent
arms

of beach
grass

glyph
the sand

faint
whorls

around
each stem

traces
of speech

§

stenographer
of earth
i interview
the land

a camera
this small room
my eye

§

every
where
i walk

fox trots

§

dozens of
sea urchins
dropped by
gulls beaked
open sucked
out

§

The sound
(SURE)
of trees wind
& surf

rhythm of
my steps

the silence
to the world
outside

when i stop

blood cruising
to the gills

the hollow
thunk of
wave on rock

ear & eye
the radiant
receivers

§

this western wind
lures me on

body follows
obedient

§

star root
of driftwood

blacked &
twisted

like a
starfish

points my
way

§

Sea Broth
a sketch
DROSS

§

the quiet cove
inside Overset

behind the
breakwater

no swells
only wind
ripples

runs on the
surface

the black
spine of
Overset

§

unable to

find the path
again
through the
woods
to Wreck
Cove

i ponder
a moment

pick up
fox's track

he leads
me where
i want
to go

§

spindrift
in the cove

the procession
of a wave

steady into wind

giving up a bit
off the top

but steady
all the way
to shore

§

just one
part
of the ocean
swells

liquid
shudder

around
the edge
& still

any wave
any shore

it's all the
same but

never will
happen
again

§

Wreck Cove
a horizontal
stone arch
at low tide
banks of rock
& shots of foam
all broken
here —

a morass

limbs of trees
shells, birds
shards of glass

the water
pounds
in from
open sea

lady's slipper
crab backs
clusters of
mussel fisted
kelp black spiders
broken traps
buoys warp
lines floats
urchin shells
yellow moss
a coat or
boot pine cones
lathes lighters
bottles caps
a net

spongy back
dump
bulldozed
by the sea

§   **margin**

from these
cliffs sea
weed
plants

below
sway in
the surf

above
these
cliffs

sumac
& low
brush
sway
in wind

waves
of each
growth

foam
spume
snow

§

the view from
a cave out
of the cold

Outer Green
distant black
spine slow
surf train
cormorant roost
home
to duck

the seas a
surf all
around
eiders swells
of ocean tides
white shoals
on the horizon

an eider
lifts his
chest
from water
with flapping
wing white
breast

tender surf
& i'm caught
in words

it's such
a simple
thing
this ball
of rock
& water

SEA KNUCKLE

KELP SKIN

all life
on or in

perceive
the rest

i come
complete
not in
pieces

i build
the nest

sand
stone
weeds

§

clamshell
tight swell
of living bone
lumped hinge
beginning
of house / home
for salty flesh
successive
orbits of
calcified
wings
glazed in-
side

§

or stain
of fox
piss
in the
snow

§

this apple tree
on the side
of the island
where it falls
to the sea
how its
branches
all bend
into the hill
trying to scramble
back up the
side

or wind

it is
the wind
off the sea
that's shaped
it so

rounded
it into
the hill
into the land
to survive

§

now my
step ascending
how my body

bends into it
trudging home

§

I saw a
cormorant
do flips
in the air
twice
  &
crows
crest on
a draft
headline
into the
cove

§

run off
granite
blocks

outcropping
from the
earth

exposed sides
& island
flanks

sun/snow
melt

dripping
sound
drop by
drop

a sea

§

behind me
a marsh
dry pale
stalks of
cat o' nine
tails
spikes
with soggy
corn stalks
the soft tan
fibers
left to
the wind
brackish
water

§

i don't
write

like fox
i ex-
perience

CAPERS

in the
cauliflower
surf

CATALYST

§

clam shells
on the beach
at low tide

large white
gaping mouths

speechless
in beauty

having outlived
the use of
tongues

§

Overset

walking
your back
i am an element
of wind

emit sounds
startle at
my own voice

runoffs
nothing's
the same

sea swell
surf fluid
broth
spume

spin drift
in my brain

wave cycles
rounding
it off

& i'm
possessed

can't stop
gawking

§

surf on
the boundary
shore

heaves
& sighs

swells full
brows over
breaks

in sweet

release

the white foam
of union

the slight
thunders
of love

§

quartz veined
rock ribbed
bulks of granite
i sit & watch
the wind below
scuttle the bay
like passing
thought

§

gaggles of
birch in
clumps

the quiet
close alder
scrawls

interjection
of winter weeds

interruptions
of stone

soft ex-
clamation
of spruce &
fir

exhortation
exhalation
elations
of elm

the warm
hoarse
juniper

jack pine
dwarf

felt antler
of sumac

i ascend
the stair

barbed
quotes of
black
berry

§

whip me
wind

lick me
dry

wet in
the arms

of Overset

i accept
ocean

as my
savior

§

slant sun
as i crest
the hill

gravel crunch
under my boots

the quiet
around

the sounds
of my body

clothed / naked

hurrying home

§

i spy
the tip
of Over-

set
where
once
i put him
up by
surprise
coming
around
the tip
into wind

my sound
muffled
by water
& wind

his hot
scramble
off the
rocks

& outta
the sun

§

at night phosphorescence
in the surf

by day
spindrift off
the lee end
of Overset

rainbow flare
western sun

§

ice melt
spills down
the beach
among
the dross
a river
gorge
flowing
in song
back to
sea

§

hawks
aloft
in the
raucous
wind

here on
the beach

& i
grounded

heart still
in their
shadow

§

while the wind

thrashes the limbs
of an alder
the empty nest
holds fast

but no birds
fly today

no boats ply
the featherwhite
waves

§

grass tussocks
on dunes behind
a field of
sand & grass
swales
to shallow
fringe forest
growth
white line
of clashing
confluent
waves

large chowder
shells

suck & draw
a wedge of
sand

BRINE LINES

waves ram
the shore

white popping
bubbles of surf
sand pocking

§

there's no
philosophy
in all
of this

any path
i try
fox has
walked

it's only
me
following

§

the skeleton
of a mushroom
dome

trees & brush
strong rooted
gathered together

ropes into
the earth

TIED/TIDE
down
low

CURIOS

it's the remains
the buckling
down & in
that counts

to stand
alone the
winter
wind

are the
rocks
cropped

cover me
with snow

i absorb
sun
shatter
the moon

"i wake
you stone
love this
man"

§

& now

back to
the greening
path

an easier
step a
surer pace

i've sur-
vived
the descent

wend my
way

home

§

saying my
solitary
farewells

strange
this is
not where
i would
have thought
i'd end up

sitting on
this rock
at the far
end of Sing-
ing Beach

but this is
indeed
the end

from here
every step
is a step
away –
begins the
long trudge
home

Birth Song: for my wife & my daughter

i

AIR

early spring
in the north
cold night
wind

logs in
the hearth
on fire

i sit
brooding
clouds
of smoke

sparks
& stars
in the
fathering
air

ii

WATER

restless
she sleeps
alone

she seems
to cradle
a sea
in her hips

a flood
of waves
in the blood
swell after
quickening
swell
into the canal
crests &
breaks

she wakes

up on her
elbows
face flush
& grim
whispers
the word
urge is
push

breath
caught &
held

the hissing
wave of
release

iii

EARTH

foam white
you ride
the tide

out of
the womb
into the bay
of waiting
hands

my fingers
frame
the flesh
feel
the plates
shift in
the squeeze
of birth

you crown

head tender
cradled
shoulders
like capes
caught on
the main

tears & strain
the burning
stretch of
flesh & pain
a slight
turn
& earth
with a final
push

sweet release
the sudden
rush

into my hands
you sea blue
flecked with
foam

naked new
wet land
at last

iv

FIRE

laid trailing
your cord
onto the
breast
we coo you
into breath
hushed
a girl

all energy
that earth
& sky
can bare
focused
on you
piece
of flint
spark
we hold
into the palms
of our
hands

passages clear
you sputter
seem to catch
each new
breath
like bellows
kindles fire
colors your
flesh

you begin
to glow

v

ISLANDS

suspended
how you
depend
your cord
back to
earth

poor drowned
land
as the weight
of birth
lifts
she rises

the waters
of care
run off
her sides
& you nurse

there

cord
clamped
& cut
an island
unto
yourself

bask in
the warmth
of the outer
world
as we
ease down
mend in
the union
that brought
you here

vi

MAPS

the tugs
to deliver
placenta
map of your
beginnings
this too
scanned
& found
intact
carried to
the back
garden

quiet dig
iron spade
tang of
steel bowl
the smell
of birth
everywhere
in the night
air

i pound
my hands
stamp
my feet
a small dance
alone on
the turned
ground

a man's
need to
husband
the seed

what fed
one
will feed
us all

vii

NAMING

we want
something
of the awe

the hush of
your birth

something
native
of blood in
the soil

sea hewn
one
we name
you

Shawnee
Marie

viii

PRAYER

daughter
take flight

from
the nest
of our
hands

from the
crotch &
the tree

rise &
fly free

The Bar Harbor Suite

for Carol
for life – again

§ PROLOGUE

Bluenose (as
the story goes)

is where
  our trip
      began

We came
in fog
left
in sun

One way round
the Loop
thru the harbors

N'East
  S'West
    Seal

On our way
to Unity

Harmony &
Freedom

§

vagabond

mist in
the light
outside
our window

tonight
in the flat
lands

a house
afloat

in a field
of fog

§

overlook

purple asters
& pigeons
on the rocks

behind
the souvenir
shop

the float
where ACADIA
moors
      empty
in autumn

  NO WHALES
WATCH TODAY

only asters
purple pigeons
on the rocks

§

pick ups

modern
fishers
of (wo)men
beefed up
with stereo
cruising
the main
drag

deep
sea eyes
sweep
the harbor
streets

gonna
set out

some nets
tonight

gonna
make a
haul

§

in the
galleries
under glass

polished brass

scrimshaw
coral anemone
junk glazed
pot

It's all re-
collection

says the
Platonist
potter

Don't worry
This is only
a memory

of what went
before

§

view from
cadillac

the village
where we were
just moments
ago the shops

small islands
caped in fog

the Porcupines

Bald   Burnt

Long   Sheep

where D'Iberville
played osprey
to the English
herring

today
the whiter
wings

of friendship
sloops

swoop over
Frenchmans
Bay

§

off shore

for Estaban
Gomez (1525)
& the rest

it's only
land

it means

to give
it up

to plant
a seed

one's foot

now we go
pedestrian

§

on the road
to cadillac

perched atop
pink granite
i'm caught

two peregrines
playing in wind

the tiercel skies
wings like scythes
parting the air
he waits

on his mate
wings over
in a fierce
stoop

raspy cackles
as they clasp
talons

roll about
& break away
again

slate & ice

reckless alchemy
of arctic air

quick in their
bearing
       straight
to the south

i stare
after them

stare
    until
only air
remains

air &
the after-
image
of their
passage

in
the sea
of my
being

a wake
in my
heart

§

Stacey's
Variety Show
is on the air

Bluegrass
Yankee style

but when some kid
from Downeast
sings the S'West

(I'd walk
across Texas
for you)

he loses
his voice

Take it boys

motel commercials
colonial furniture

Later &
closer
to home

pipes &
fiddles

those Nova
Scotia nights

§

Thistle Patch
        Farm

I remember
days of rain

Hard Rain

Like a cow
pissing

on a flat
rock

§   **2 Found Poems**

i

Snow?

Do you get
much snow

here – in
Maine

I mean?

ii

My country
is not

a country
It is snow

My garden
not a garden
but a white
plain

My road

is not
a road

It is only
snow – here

in Maine
I mean

§ Commotion at
Sand Beach

He skirting
in a widening
arc – arms out

his barefeet
stuttering
in the sand

trying to get
the damned thing
to stand still

pose for waddling
camera-faced wife

The maverick gull
won't fly – he
wants my food

(finally)

It's OK
Herb

I don't
have

any film
left

anyway

§   **the clasp**

Before
we bank

into parting
sleep

we pause
in our flight

Like pilgrim
birds

just passing
thru

we clutch
& tumble

in the mid-
night air

§

she says it
reminds her
of the Cape

the galleries
the craft places

asleep now
nestled in
the hollows
of my limbs

building bridges
into the night

§   EPILOGUE: TRINITY

I place
our bodies
against the land

She – S'West
to my N'East
& this youngest
Seal – or so
she seemed to us
waiting in silence
at the breath-hole
as we charmed her
from our waters
into our air

Or call it
by name – you

joyful song
& I rock

we three
seal rock song
Unity

where Route 3

runs into

1

.

Poems in Magazines, 1988-1992

§   ox of earth

twitching
wild cherry
out of the woods
logs locked
under each arm
drumming the earth
back into my bones

this is timbre
i can dance to

3 weeks here
& i finally

arrive

§ SPRINGSPUNS

1

old man
with boy

on a bench
in Lincoln Park

that foun-
tain again
(into air)

PIGEONS
SPRING

2

they are waiting
for me

as i round
the corner

3 winos
standing
in sun

SPRING
(their trap)

3

young couple
too young
he seems

right now
i'm inside
his laugh

how does
it feel

her breast
THIS SPRING

4

dogwood blossoms
on Congress Street

old women

in white gloves

O My Laundry
Queens

madonnas
in the park
their perfect
children

SPRING
from their
laps

§   **to Jane**

I thought
you might
come

I went
to the beach
to gather
wood

you may
stay late

§   **bag man**

I'm surprised
to find

a sea
of pigeons

in a side
street

parking
lot

until i
remember

yesterday

THE RUSSIAN

with a gym
bag

fullacrumbs

§

the silver
diaphanous
spider web

throbs in
the wind

on a barbed
wire fence

§

around
the clipped
asters

in the jar
on the porch

love lingers
like a bee

The quarry:west end:long island:fall 1990

§

the dark
elderberry
clusters
outside
the window
a scatter
of growth
leaves &
needles
woodsmoke
rising from
deep inside

§

monarchs still
in early autumn
above the brown
spikes of mullein
the split pods of
milkweed flatten
their wings bob
in the breeze
that lifts
from the sea
driftfall over
the quarry rim
more glide than
flutter down
the rock face
onto the floor
yarrow stalks
& goldenrods

§

the constant
churring
of crickets
under the
dry juniper
berries
the pink
hop clover
bees work
the asters
the bright
rose hips
butterflies
everywhere
pale yellow &
black jittery
flight or
sudden pounce
light in
the grass
& just
as fast
out again
& gone

§

a quiet
exchange
undercurrent
of cricket
background of
slack tide

a stillness
anticipation
of change as
a leaf falls
the sound
of earth
breathing
my breath

§

i drowse
in clover
ants cover
me a beetle
dragonfly
on my face
i am claimed
in the grass
my shallow
roots lie still
in the silence

§

flight by
directed whim
antic of wind
featherbrains
in a torrent
of thought
routes & paths
an airy maze
where they

always seem to
second guess
themselves

§

grasshoppers
one smaller
& green
on the back
of a larger
brown
caught
in the act
under my eye
as still
as andirons
in the burning
grass

§

the trembling
awkward walk
of daddy long
legs on drift
wood in the
dry grass one
leg feeling
along the limb
the quiet ponder
of trail taken
or delicate probe
what lies beyond

§

why should
goldenrods
be growing out
the tops of
the highest
rocks the bulk
of the point
marooned stalks
wedged in small
pockets of stone
a butcher's block
for seagulls
crab backs &
urchin shells
pecked open
ground down
rough soil
for seed
up for grabs
it's too easy
to say it's life
roots down
sucking stone
yet i do

§

flying
grasshopper
a flick
& a whir
black wings
snapped out
in the wind

a dark cape
lined with
gold dust

§

autumn
all one
alone
all
in all
such a
private
act

§

basking
on a rock
it is the
tide now
the water
seeks me out
cold arms
of it or
foaming lip
over lip
over sand
over foot
engulfed
in such a
loving act

§

an exquisite
hour hunched
in front of
the fire
no movement
except my eyes
out the door
out the windows
hawk on
a post
alone with
his eye
his hungry
heart

§

how ripe
& full the
world seems
a thick wax
sheen on all
the leaves on
all the plants
flowers in
their boldest
statements
rich lacquer
of late sun
clarity of
sea & air
a clean edge
to everything
this is

the wine of
harvest time
the deep sap
of all things
distilled
in the globe

Green Heart

§

picture
a boy

standing
on a pier

staring in
to the sea

today
face pressed
to glass

a man
flies back
against
that sun

lost again
in those same
deep blues

§

full moon
on the wing
tip

this flight
homes

through
the moist
white air

§

wobbling
on my pivot

alone
at home

love
at the
poles

this idle-
ness

between

§

on this
wheel

I would
press

the world
back

with my
thumbs

create
a place
for us

a hollow

space

you & i
just inside

the rim

§

your call
overdue

i look

make sure
the phone

is still
on the hook

§   (h)our

say we were
   together
      once in time

like the hands
   of a clock
      at noon

rooted to that
   same center

i have come
full circle

my minute
  movements

around
  the face

climb back
  toward you

approaching
  once again

or slightly
  thereafter

§

phone ringing
  in the still
  night air

a quick finger
flicking crystal

  i quiver
  & quiet

  your words
  pour in

§   **Singing Beach
Manchester, Mass.**

i walk between
the rock arms

of this raw cove

shoulders hunched
against the wind

eyes down
on moonshells
& fishbones
i spy

a late bloom
of brilliant
beach-pea

two new
crescent
leaves

curl back
to one stem

GREEN HEART

alone
in acres
of sand

this life
warms

§

crisp
October
night

moon:
a tipped
bowl

leaves fall

sounds
of small
animals

fill the
woods

§

i dance alone
in the spilled light

an apparition
in my arms

Yellow Aster Butte

§

the soft
colors belie
the hard
cliffs i
want
to wear
weave a
fabric
my body
inside
a land-
scape of
moss & stone
shores
of it
around
my neck
sleeved in trees
my limbs
protrude
wear this
mountain
a while
move on

§

the pure
geometry
of climbing
the inclined
planes
the cones
above the

meadow
flats
the physics
of walking
hiking up
through
the bones
through
the sinews
muscular
breath
& blood
we strive
to rise
above
the slash
four of us
a foot
at a time

§

full
moon
bowl
in the
day sky

pouring
bounty
on to
the earth

source
of the

south
wind

Tomyhoi
Peak

§

rivulets of trees
on the slopes
above & around
the alpine
meadows
like flocks grazing
against the
grass along
the rockslides
the rich colors
of deep autumn
of blueberry
lowbush &
crimson
splotches of
pale yellow
lighter greens
& reds
after frost
evergreen
along the
brows, the
rock outcrop
random
or is it
the few
who hold

to the top
losing distinction
with distance
into snow
peaks &
steep shadow

§

among
the pale
purple
asters
a perfect
half circle
of stones
in the
pool
the rust
of machinery
apt in its
burnished
autumn color
the slick
steel of
spring

gold it
was whole
hills
burned off
stripped
away
peeled back
like skin
scabbed

over
over
the years

sun on
the water

the only
gold
in sight

§

hawk over
the peak
unmoving
subtle shifts
like a shaft
of wind
its shadow
over the ground
black
banded
tail swift

shrewd
the wisdom
of movement
in its element
air opens
hawk seems
to just
enter

§

go up
there

eat our
apple

on the
peak

before
it's too

late

§

the flicking of
grasshoppers
in the brush
as my feet
push on
the path

§

cairns
the little
piles
of stone
men make

§

a dusky
hawk
sweeps
down
the slope

& through
the meadow
where we
sit

a shaft
of wind
he works
the land
a foot –
no more
above
the ground

his sharp
black shadow
flags behind

that dark
self
that rags
us all

§

silent shafts
flanks
thrown up

& back
against the
sun a rigid
sprawl
bare hefts
of stone
washed
clean or
streaked
mounts
brows of
evergreen
stillness
in wind

§

jagged
sound
of bird
call
punctures
of the
wind
maroon-
ed

§

burned off
the trees
to expose
the land
get into

the guts
for gold

§

in the distance
snow flanks
white facets
in the Frasier
Valley in
the distance

§

rivers
of snow
among
the crags

the darker
washes
of valleys

silver
threads
of spider
webs

disappear
into air

whatta
ride

§

small birds
the delicate
feathers
hollow bones
alive up-
lifted song

§

my mouth
a cave
in wind

a dull
hollow
sound

how to
shape

to say
anything

one to
another

this word
or that

§

how wind
slithers

through
grass

trail
that leaves
no trace

scarf

§

the fabric
of snag
broken off
the sinews
still show
winding
around
in place
ascent
done

§

the descent
into the
wind
a dusky
hawk
tossed
up who
survives
made for
this
movement

§

against
the grain
of all
we stand
for
against
our pose
so temporary
upon the
peak

§

a blank
page
spires
against
the sky
or black
scratches
on a
white
page
who
creates

§

a fin
or
a
blade
the

color-
ful
skin
on this
peak

§

earth
protrudes
the light
reaches
out from
raspberry
ridges
spiked
with deep
green

huddled
below

the gray
blade
splotched
w/ lichen

§

contours
of color
molded
around
or into
the land

these
rough
outcroppings
will there
be time
enough
for it
all
the dance
of a blade
of grass
staccato
in wind
pulsing
from a
rooted
foot

§

in the
shadow
of late
afternoon
sharply
defined
reds
rivers

definition
shadow
& sun

the distilled
liquid of
afternoon

sun a
glaze

§

sky reflected
copper & bronze
in pools below
          us

a stream
of boulders

roughnecks

the darker
sides of
evergreen
against the
ghost (sharp)
backdrop or
background
the sun
somewhere
in between

§

swaths of
clearcut
below
slain
valleys
dull &
supine

chicken
scratch
cross hatch
dull life-
less glisten

the democratic
growth
higher
fallen as
the body
labors down
a deep
quivering
in the
thighs

§

how like
dogs these
mushroomers
off the trail
on knowing
impulse
eyes like
noses
to the ground

§

Lance's
laughter
stone mushroom
a table

of ——
for the
table to-
night
King Boletus
steinpilz
as he
whips out
his blade
CHOICE

§

the sound
of water
in the
flats
½ way up/
down
where
water
mingles
joins to-
gether
in its
descent

how it
meanders
through
this meadow
& is gone
underground
later on
the trail
louder &

much longer
increased
color & life
counter-
point to
the gathering
shade

§

the mind
given over
becomes
the maker
of paths

how to
arrive

roots &
feathers
underfoot

§

splashing
water
cool clear
bells
of it
wind
tinning
rills
over rocks
a hand-

full
mouth to
my body
a lake
inside

§

wings
incised
on the
skin
of the
boletus
tents
etched
on the
pale
dome
men
of an
earlier
time
antlers
& moons
in the meat
we'll eat
this
flesh
Lance
breaks
off
offers
up
in the
fine

wine
of these
woods

§

roots like
veins, bones
of stone
far country
trilling
in the
throat
of wind
striking
bird song
the back
of my
ear

§

a dollop
of moss
over a
hollow
in the
tree
Bertha
reaches
in
pitch &
limbs
solidified
pulled

out a
tree being
hand
upraised
in greeting
knotty
pitch eyes
up turned
mouth

§

what silence
is there

more silent
than this

the human
voice

calling back
over
the trail

& after
the echo

no re-
sponse

§

we descend
through

layers of
wind
the hotter
breath
of lower
land
back to
stumps
where fir
grows a-
gain

not in
but through
the forest
roads
not paths
she says

§

how dull
this lowland
vista con-
fusion can't
see the
forest
for . . .
a road
airplane
slash in
the clear
cut the
smooth
gleaming
steel of

automobiles
or heavy
machinery
grinding gears
fertilizer pellets
where forest
service signs
warn against
the picking
of wildflowers
sedge & grass
Yellow Aster
Trailhead

Enjoy
Do Not Destroy
Your American
  Heritage

Elegy

§

sailor
you emerged
as out
of a fog
i knew
your eyes
before i
saw your
face heard
your words
before
you spoke

a woman
the bridge
between us

i see
the sails
snap up
in her eyes
when she
puts out
upon the deep

a sense
of loss
as here

& yet
i've learned
to loose
the hawsers
of my heart

buoyed
in the solace
of a common
mooring

a haven of
still water
& stowed sails

the berth of
kindred blood
that runs
in our veins

honored be
the women
who love
the earth
& care for
her men

who cradle
hulls out of
the water
ready for
the greater
passage

ashes cast
to the wind
like sails
like words
like breath

i stand
rooted to
this shore

my eyes
strain
into the sun
for dark
shapes
under
the sea
for one man
adrift
on the deep
sailing in
his way
such a
solitary
act

i have scanned
the charts
i too
carry
something
of the black
cargo in
my hold
gems & ashes
alone on
the sea
of any man's
being

i see
you cut
through
the waves
driven by
our breath
well on

your way
to whatever
we know
of a godly
isle

Descending Down to My Roots I Sing

1

mussel shells
& eel grass
smooth pieces
of wood in
the pocking
surf arcs
of dry spume
tracks in
the dark sand

a small rock
for my pocket

scuffing along
the surf line

2

beach of
dri ki &
deep surf

my lady
in white
walking
higher up
the beach

contemplating
with her foot
now her hand

an armful
of driftwood

for her garden
in another
land

3

a single cloud
caught against
the green ridge

shifts in wind
not what it was
where or who

but how this
cloud caught

plays out
its solitude

4

white feathers
sprawl in
the wet sand

crosshatch of
gull tracks
tangled coils
of kelp

this is the
western sum
of all i've
ever seen

swirling arcs
small tongues
white in
the backwash

the pale fronds
of cedar boughs

5

one loon in
the broad cove

a solid point
of black & white

rides the waves
lifts his wings

emblem of the
incoming tide

6

the land
cut —
trees cut

black trunks
on the hillside

a feather
in whose

cap

7

lineage

old growth
& the human
body

limb
to limb

on the
autumn
beach

8

walking the trail
to botanical beach

a rock spine
through the
salt woods

wet puddles
stop to look
finger the
fine buds

how you doing
deep inside

9

suddenly cool

near the shore

moist & shady
moss & vines

spires of
tall & slender
poplars

rise from
the muck

reach for
the sun

10

sounds
of water
& bird
calls
open at
the end
streams
meet the
sea trees
give over
to grass
swales

CAUTION
Pacific Coast
Rogue Waves
& Swells

11

sediment wall
stories high
from sea floor
all tan & sand
whole rocks
exposed in
the hard flanks
under roots
pockets of
red berries
in the cliff
side a small
dark hole
a chink &

a pale fern
goes it
alone

12

this magnif-
icent
wall weeps

from a
crevice

wet runs
down the
cheeks

13

away from
the noise
of the surf

water rises
currents tug

silent at
the still
pools

14

hanging in
space it seems
the trunk &
roots of risen
cedar tentacle
the cliff face
marble veins
strain moss
in vertical
growth from
vertical planes
dark & spongy
stuff heavy
with the smell
of spawn
brooding ground
for the raucous
crow

15

we're all
rocks washed
the rippled
sun water
back to
the source

16

underfoot
soft dross
the panning
of pebbles
the charred
spine of
oak the
iron stem
rust on
the rocks
chipped &
faded red

17

sink your
teeth
into this

clench
& mull

what coast
this is

boats ply
in bands
of white
bands of
gray or

the open
meat of
sea & sky

18

crow rising
from limb
to limb

shadow alive

did you
ever see

schist
thrust

crows low
in the flyways
of the forest

black wings
cutting close

did you
ever see

wilder
land

19

sift & yield
steady flow
as persistent
as soft rain
around & under
anyway the cycle
back to the sea
back to sound

20

breath
of a
bird

legs a-
long a
tidal
pool

flock
wings

soft
pedaling
beak

threading
away at

the fabric
of air

21

sea line
dark whelks
& kelp beds

pink & purple
rockcrust

delicate the
pale limpets
stuck in ovals

barnacles &
mussel shells

clinging
closed up
covered by

the mother
of waves

22

jolt of
bracing wind
holes in
the rocks
hard shells
breathe
inch along
in their
briny lung

slow   slow

the dance

swaying
to the pulse
of the ocean
drum

23

fitting
our fingers

in hollows
of stone

this
    rock

i
    thee

wed

24

shell heaps
in a stone
fire pit

i drive
crows off
with only
my eyes

a shelter

of driftwood
laid up
on the shore

plank tables
& stump chairs
a raft of logs
for a roof

edge of
the forest

edge of
the sea

i leave

as others
before me

crows
descend

25

eagle off
the point

above the
trees slow
circles on
the wind

old surf
tail

an old
creation
tale

26

on leaving
the beach
the same crow
the same low
arcing flight
from the cedar
on the point
long hefts
over the waves
down the beach
tips up
lights
near the
forest edge
lands

27

on her
lips

a deep
taste

dark &
tart

heart
in mouth

soaked in
brine

28

away from ocean
the surges less
the pulses less

scent wafts
across the trail
insect noise
small birds
appear

the earth
hunkered down
held in sway

away from
the shore

leaves fall

29

no caterwaul
of kids
island small
ferns maybe
thousands
of miles
released
from home
or late sun

that walk
back from
South Side
East Coast
years ago
our youth

30

fields of
stumps &
fireweed

scabs &
sutures on
the earth

Planted
in '66

Thinned
in '86

Jordan River
Dangerous
Currents

Public Be
Warned

Managed Land

Point
No
Point

31

what ship
is this

orange moon
splits the clouds
lifts her sails

a wake
of light
chaliced
on the
sea

funneled

a vortex
of gold

shimmers
to the
shore

32

soft plashing
of small waves
calm without
pattern tonight

random gulls
land in
the moon's
light

33

herons
in the
night
air

the bay

shallow

stalkers

take a
stand

34

full of
our own
tides

pull of
the moon

we come
together

in the
fish camp

at dawn

35

black crows
on black wires

the full moon
blanched white

silhouettes
of gulls
in the pale
pastels
of dawn
water

one other
man alive

fishing time
he says with
a rising smile

36

madroña
like veins
in the
morning
sun behind
the eye
carrying
greenery
fifty years
i've come

to this
my peeled
bark half
century
beauty
rooted
to earth
turned to
the sun
this season
brings me
from my
aspirations
back to
earth i
cry like
crow crow
like cock
descending
down to
my roots
i sing

Poems in Manuscript

§ Shooting Squirrels

i

There seems to be no one else alive
except the dog that nods in sun and the cat
that eyes him from the parlor window.

Five years ago I watched hawks
high in the sky above this porch.

Today one small bird against these winds.

ii

I remember rifle shots on the shore of Eagle Lake.
An old guide's son was sitting as quietly
as I am right now   shooting squirrels.

iii

When I was a boy
I used to get skins from a friend
who hunted squirrels with his father.

Stiff pelts of grey white fur   tails intact.
Parchment backs of scraped flesh.
Vein words stacked dry.

iv

These fathers and sons.
And squirrels here that run the wires.

This squirrel in front of me
I whistle to a stop.   Cock my eye.

§ christian

i have to smile.
you dropped
the marbles
on the floor
picked them up
before bed

and now
while you sleep
i see two
a red and
a yellow
under the table
behind the chair

and yet at times
you see in your mind
what i often
dare guess
like the night
i read to you
my audience of one
you listened and said
"peter, the wind
is really alive."

§

Christian
caught hell today
fell in a puddle
coming home
from school
hear him

in the other room
telling his brother
"a dog drowned
in that puddle
yesterday.
He's buried
right now.
Drowned in
my puddle."

§   **missing work on a Monday morning**

for K.K. on vacation

I don't remember looking
knowing you wouldn't be there.
I didn't even lift my head
heavy with rain, weariness.

I stood on the corner waiting
for a bus I supposed hadn't come.
But you weren't there to signal me.
I had no urge to run this
morning. No urge to go at all.

Staring hard into passing cars
I realized the bus had come and gone.
And when it came again I knew
what I was going to do.
I'd be like you – not there!
Not waiting. Not this morning.

§   **Congress Square**

the old woman
dropped a dime

she didn't move

it was as if
like the years
it was gone

until he
bent down
& picked it up

the return
was infinitely
slow

they never
touched

§   **dream**
        for chris

it was
the kind
of joy
that comes
from fairy
tales

comic
round

full of fun
rolling
as laughter
through
my flesh

§

sitting
in the office

early sunday
morning

perched
on my chair

my chest out
beating

because

the only other
moving things

in these
4 blocks

are pigeons

flying

into sun

§   **portrait of a lady**

Jesus!
Whatta Broad!

STANLEY CUP CHAMPS

bright   orange

on her chest

a portrait of
the entire
BOSTON BRUINS
hockey team

Pads & All

1971

§   Kevin

he enters
subdued

'are you
going to
spank me?'

sitting alone
at the table

feet dangling
a foot from
the floor

he eyes
his prize

over warmed-
over beans

an eel
in a soda
bottle

fog-damp
sniffles

'i hope
i find
a pail'

§

Could i
git a
dime?

Gotta
git in
outta
the cold

i know
you guys
don't have
much

just
a little

Gotta
git in
outta
the cold

for him
yes – you

i don't
know

§ Kevin's Appaloosa

That's my favorite horse
hanging on the wall.
He's white – paper white
with red and black lakes
all over his hide –
a long black tail
a single blue eye.

Jesus – I'd like to
tangle my fingers
in your fine black mane
and ride you wild
across the sky –
Night Ride! Night Ride!

§ West Branch Penobscot

all day
fishing
wets & drys

in the river
in the sun

night
as i close
my eyes

i see
the river
still

what rise
what rise

§

midnight moon
shadows
follow me
across sand

i voice
my song

waves come
around my feet
salt against
my lips

***

i saw
a fire
across
the sound

a shape
uncertain
touched by
moon

heard my voice
one with bells
at sea

left
my fingers
in the sand
smelling salt
touching sea

§ Will That Be All Sir?

DOWN
in the valle
where you worked

i watched
our waitress

(had seen her
before)

waiting for you
       in her

to recognize me

§ offering

On this
log
i put
3 shells

i do not
care to
keep

place
2 nails

i wish
to leave

§

Bleary Bum

BHIKKU

kerouac
   in knapsack

for young
   girls leer

black whispers
   sisters

     kerouac
     at the
     automat

   ***

it's Kerouac

coming into
this harbor
in fog

lonely men

on solitary piles
of evening wharves
fishing at dusk

wine / bagged
at their
sides

§

kevin –
on his dixie cup garden

"the li-
ma beans

YES

the ra-
dishes

NO"

§

october gulls

close shadows

on sand

at noon

***

from where i sit
i hear

one son singing

gulls
a dog
bees

you breathing
at my side

the crush of feet
in sand behind us

(silhouettes)
low voices

***

women with
dried flowers

transparent weeds

leavings
of the year

***

island in fall
like a grave
yard / cemetery

people wander
between boats

quiet insect / air

clear air
real death

***

the smallest sound
like an arrow

through air

colors leaves with
the year / as we
pick up & go

so gathers she

perhaps we too
should attend
our dead
this way

   ***

it passes
in clarity
& beauty

stripped
bare
before
the cold

vintage / harvest

i shadow
on miles
of beach

   ***

milkweed

like pine cones
or plumes of smoke

like hair
you say

like an eagle
scalloped brown

head feathers
white wings

in flight

like thick tadpoles
head / seed
trailing tail

swim through
autumn air

§   **Seasons**

in town
old women
whisper
in restaurants
pasted like
leaves

along
the aisles

it is
the dead
of winter

***

the trees
of winter
stand more
still
waiting for
the waters
of spring

***

dunes
dry eel
grass

geese
oar south
in arrow-
heads

brittle
season
of wind

time of
paring
close to
bone

§   patty's poem

i wake
to the world

like wind

searching

for you

outside
my sleep

§

c'mon
let's go
my shoes
my-
            self

        i

my name
&   me

that's all
i got
to bring

i'm goin'
to the

island

§

i slump
in my chair

in front
of the fire

i seem to be
all lips & legs

heavy-lidded

like a frog
on the nod

CHURRUMPPPP
CHURRUMPPP

***

for you
i become
bird

hair/feathers
arm/wings

cock of eye
i   cock

cockwalk
watch

my incredible
dance

FTHURRRRRR
FTHURRRRRR

THURUMPPPP
FTHURRRRRR

§

i am
a dog

HOWL
afterall

is all
i know

§   **Conversation Pieces**

christian –

raspberries
& rain

sure are
yummy

   ***

michael –

i'd like
to know

ALL
     of the birds
MOST
     of the flowers
& HALF
     of the trees

on this

island

***

christian –

    phooey
they sure
    don't make
    root beer barrels

like they used to

***

on the blackboard
at north school

joy   man   joy
peace man peace

i love
you

    angel

§   **Owen**

i sit here
lost in beer
& music

slowly aware
of your grin
on my face

no teeth
showing
just lips
& cheeks

Owen
in your
6 years

you have
nothing

going for
you

& still
you grin
Laurel's
grin

to the
face
of your
world

§   **Deanna**

for you
at 8

i was just
another man

to be charmed
& won

a fish caught
& played

but alive
in the play

our life
was the tension
of the line

it was never
resolved
who catches
is caught

§   Lunchbreak at an LD Seminar

i

i sit
on a stump
behind a tree

in front of me
an empty base-
ball field

ii

if i keep
my eyes
low enough

all i see
are dandelions

if i listen
hard

birds & wind

iii

i wait
to be confined

in dead-
lier air

david age 7
said it best

"pete

every-
body's
got to
die

once

in a
while"

§

She left
every man
she loved
but one

He beat her

to the crunch

cracked rib
a broken nose

his anxious
gestures
into space

she vortex
earth's whirlpool

i come out
the other end

§

the same table
night after night

the same sketch
(comedian)

with platinum blond
in london fog
slowing traffic
outside

cruising man
says get in

just before she
passes the bar

§

weary/one
hand
    on her hip

gives shape
    underneath

a woman
so soft

who's lost
    in an amulet
around her neck

violin strains
    down under
    her skirt

§

we at
the bar
are all
angles

colleens
laughter
(being
round)

rolls up
& over
or bursts
on edges

as sharp
as any
razors

§

    i

autumn
all one
i swim
alone
all
in all
such a
private
act

    ii

basking
on a rock
it is the
tide now
the water
seeks me out
cold arms
of it or
foaming lip
over lip
over sand
over foot
engulfed
in such a
loving act

§

i came
as deer
to open
pond

seeing
need re-
flected
there

i bolted

i have
circled

now

i watch
from far

ears
to air

nose to
ground

heart
hooves

§   **Songs**

to Jane

I thought

you might
come

I went
to the beach
to gather
wood

you may
stay late

***

for carol

you look
the same

don't know
your mind
yet

but seems
you're round
now

circular

like an
indian

lodge

***

commorant
song

shag
black

head and
neck

ass —
as he

dives

***

city

i didn't
touch
the earth
today

i didn't
even
touch
the earth

***

i had
a hard time

when i thought
that spring

would never
come

***

j

there is
something
about

not wanting
to enter

darkness
at all

you still
beside me

are just
enough

to keep me
away

***

early spring
nine blue herons
overhead

***

§

1st ray
of hope

amid the
tangle

of blackberry
spikes

rusted iron
& steel

a fall
blooming
crocus

PINK

belying its
toughness

§

blue aztec
extra early
extra sweet

planted
across
the garden

as across
the country
we came

some blues
among the
gold here

extra early
extra sweet

§

mountain
driving

rounding
a bend

at the top
of a rise

the high
beams

of my
headlights

meld with
the moon's

§

northern
cascades

broadleaf
  maples

spill their
  leaves

down the
  limbs

of hemlock
  & fir

a minor refrain
like
intermittent rain

where high
    rivers

thunder
    down

the rock
    spines

of steep
    green

slopes

§

Under the lower limbs of the cedar tree
the shed stands like an old man in a moss
green coat; its roof lapped in the old way
board and batten only against the weather.

I peel off gray planks deep veined and weak
with years of rain but salmon flesh under
the surface when boards break under the strain.

I pry rusted nails from blackened holes
my fingers undressing the shed to its frame.
Stripped and listing the bare timbers
are easy pickings for my crow bar,

In the glazed eye of a cracked window
I see the glint of my own skin

as the shed topples to its knees.

A stale breath of cobwebs and dust
and the frame falls flat to the ground.

Anxious birds flit about as I clean up
giving this space back to earth – a dark void

The gaping mouth of a cedar tree.

§

Bobby

a beer
& a
book

coat
off
con-
tent

§

goodbye

see you
in 2
years
or so

i might
have my
house

done
by then

sooner
i say
sooner

§

my aunt
Ruth (85) in
a nursing
home
only son
at sea
sitting by
a window
injured
foot up &
wrapped
reading
head aslant
Reader's Digest
large type
white wisping hair
slack freckled
face & jaw
nearly leaps
from her chair
heart jumps
in instant
recognition
(the eyes)
she says
after all these
years

§ harbor songs

cloud shadows
on clouds
below

dozing
into Maine
on the
red eye

the pale
transparent
blue

deepening
behind strata
of clouds

the flight
path
to Portland

low & over
the islands

———

white caps
kick up
& fade back
like boils

———

the breakers
on the shore

vectors of foam

in slow soft
white raking
of shallows
around
islands

scattered ships
plowing the
greater sea
the sweep
of ocean

the full
meaning
of bay

———

full salt
air off the
harbor

a white
stone
plaque-
less

Longfellow's
birth place

'vandals
took the
handle'

housed
now
who knows
where

———

gulls against
the sun faded
sky their white
wings & calls
swoop down
on the fish plant
their shadows
around me

———

the red bowed
NANTUCKET
light ship

boots & pick-
up truck
small boats
among the
big inboards

supper for 3
on the island
tonight

root my
feet in
place
again

———

Harborside
concrete & ice
the spacious
displays of
haddock cod

steamers cherry-
stones the smell
of lobsters
cooking down
the cobblestone
streets

———

it's still
the same
process

the same
ropes thrown
by the same
men

we're
moored
from the
same sea

thick ropes
on iron
cleats

———

constant
flurry &
flash
the splash-
ing water
of quarreling
gulls
swirling
whirlwinds
of feather

& noise

———

little boy
tottering
on concrete
waving his
arm after
a pigeon
reaching
to grasp this
feathered
flight

stands
still eyes
up into
the sun
wondering
why

———

sea gull
rides sideways
a slanting
drift
tacking
in the
wind
given over
to the element
complete
ease &
understanding

i don't
give a

fuck
she said

watch me
slide down
the wind

———

Bett'nany Jean
barrels through

———

sailboat floundering
in the bay
sails aflutter
sharp cracking
in wind
drops the jib

it's been
an odd
mixture
of pleasure
& pain

while an-
other full-
bellied &
sleek
breasts by

———

the pointed flight
of dusky
cormorants
by the Bug Light
heading in

———

the meditative
faces of people
ease in
their bodies
ease in
their limbs
who sit
alone
& wonder
at quiet
questions
posed by
the sea

———

wink
of an
eye

Portland
Head or
the light
at Bug
Point

finished
or raw &
undone

———

red tug
all chest
shoulders
& belly
rubber

tired tied
into the
barge

red with crane
the dredge

—let's build
a house

—a house
of stone
right here

in the middle
of this bay

———

the harried
flight of
tern – white dart
with wings
over a
green buoy
a channel
marker
off the tip
of Peaks

———

she restored
me
gave back
my blackened
soul
to light
it began

here
on this
boat in this
water

———

birch trees
out of rock
& into
air like
white veins
in the
island

———

green mottled
shores of
home

above the
dull tan
beach

the dark
lines
of seaweeds

Long Island
Casco Bay

i drink
it all
in

§

what a great
ride out
wind & sun
a constant
warmth as
we cross
the sound
the sky clear
everything
highlighted
in the late
sun the world
alive inside

———

i leave the
road quickly
walk Front
Beach the
rocks to Cove
& Red Sand
Big & Fowlers
feel i could
walk & walk
this bordering rim
walk out my
thoughts
my sickness
sure steps
to coming clean

———

away from the
rich fishwifery
of the wharves

thin poplar
leaves yellow
in the moist
brown sand drift
wood fisted
gnarled roots
wrapt in sea
weed a whole
trunk barkless
the rich swirls
of grey growth
long limbs
smooth in the
sun the texture
of sky & dry
bone an argument
laid out in
anger one night
cribwork of roots
aired out on
this shore
i walk around
eventually
lay my hands
on run them
over the bleached
bones walk to this
charred stump
a gaping
black mouth
frozen in time
all impulse
cut off
all direction
lost hulk
in the sand
a large stone

wedged
in your
heart

———

the steps
60? 75?
that lead
back to
or forward
from my yard
are gone now

the crumpled
concrete
walls of
the boathouse
of my youth
in the side
of a hill
the steep banks
of Front Beach

———

weariness
the sadness
of descent
in my mind
back over the
years i'm on
an edge
with you

———

"eventually
you gotta
come out

in some-
body's
yard"

———

the lush banks
of vine & green
brush the dry
grass the yellow
ivy that pushes
down over the
banks onto rocks
tumble down
to the sea foam

———

red sand
maroon really
deep granular
& micaed
softening into
pink where
dry feathered thru
with drain lines
& wrinkles
shiverings of
whiter strands

———

the steady drift
inland or out
to sea of small
clouds undone
unraveled in
the sun rent
by wind
insubstantial

mutable at last
less & less
in their passage
west

———

the pale
backs of
leaves
hands
thrown up
against
the wind

———

in the sand
shadow tracks
i leave behind
clouds leaves
wind any-
thing that
lives now
lives fully

———

gulls lift
head out
into wind
stall in
soft heart
beats of
wind drift
on all eyes

———

dull green
shocks of

beachgrass
gloss of
blueberry
bush rash
of sumac
beech med-
allions
glint in
the sun
clouds of
blue spruce
clouds
of blue
spruce

———

my view

as if
the world
(tipsy)

were flushed
with wine

spirit that
pervades

the body
of it all

———

beyond Cove
Beach the dark
barnacled
backs of
rock the drying

brown seaweed
combed inward
by the waves
clusters of blue
mussels & periwinkle
walking below
where i used
to fish

———

limpets
in a tidal
pool the rich
brown slick
all life still
& heavily shadowed
stirred by the
stuttering wind
the pink
algae
along the rim
fists of Irish
moss the small
pool heaves a sigh
in & out
its own tide

———

i love this
interplay
where water
works the sand
deltas & rills
small creeks
& ponds
cut into the
sand bed the

steady ripple
getting back
any way the
sand gives
stoked by wind
back to the
source

———

smart crows
low just over
the waves
the noisy
effort to
get back
home any way
the wind
allows
low today
just over
the waves

———

beach dusted
dry with
sand wind
balmy at sun
set no two
trees the
same hue
crickets &
steady surf

§ Coast to Hope Coast

the climate not
of my element
framed in a place
i'd not choose to hang
the words of inconsiderate
content gilt edges
on the distant ropes
it's the dark corners
inside the ring
the brass of restriction
i refrain

the pungent rain
drenches we tolerate
the achievement cough
at the columbine
streaked with smoke
outside the window
in the night sea
the half-lit limb
of a Japanese tree
lanterns me
beyond the screens
no shade too great

extricate the tooth
under the gum probe
what comfort no point
in the update lends
thermals work
the treads of rain
turned to time & space
a race of wings
can't find the sun

wind gusting rain
into solid clouds
the sound of yes
inside the cabin
sweeping over
the svelte sands
shuddering hulk
rivers of water
pouring down like
curtains fall

rain lashes under
the wing brows
great tears from
a storm inside
a tense heart
beats the hard
pelt of driven
rain wind licks
the riveted steel
mercy & little more

connected
tied together
with miles between
the years

the stretch to span
the open space
like feathers
in a bird's wing
love resides

the effort
—as here—
is to rise

we are a sea
of vapor
what is outside
heaves
takes on weight
substance sprawls
when in doubt
an anthem
of attention
why not dive
in the grip
of fall

incessant boredom
backing out
into the accident
months of macadam
the patterns of a symphony
in borders of white
mincing wings
on the waves
the fraught bulk
of whales lift
from pods epiphanies
scintillating loft
of higher light

....

light bounces flat
out & smooth
coast to hope coast
minimum thrust
on the blue cover
of woven skin
arcs of wings
caves in the crust

of the earth

who wouldn't
leap & plunge

this approach
is such
a beauty

map of
a new land
flesh of idea
thrust into
the gap
the sharp
gestures of
imagination

veins swollen
on the brow
the sweat
to understand
the doing
give it
a voice
in spite of
us all

coats & ties
at the end
of a tunnel
into the groin

turgid tongues
wrapped together

this breakup

i see a pocket
among clouds
opens
a path
a further
foray
into the
eloquence
of action
new rooms
out of
the attic
the basement
falls &
in between
a latitude
of love
unfolds
each step

a riser
each tread
a thread
to the core
a shaft of
light in
the curtains
of wind
one man
wed
to life

she makes
a brick
into a wall
a breath
of air

a prison
i exist in
the open
arches
of her
being
levitate
like blue
above the
clouds
a trickle
of air
in the back
of my throat

heart
arrowing
out

§

i

settling in
on his way
out
the sudden
jump & flashing
grin
out of sleep
naked
to say

he knows

what to say

at last
instructed
for the next
foray

ii

swimming in
the waters of words
there is a stroke
that concerns
the heart
a map
of the cold
moraine
with roads
that reach out
like veins
an infusion
he begins
to feel
settling in
on his way
out

§

no step too great
none too small
no road too empty
no thought that
isn't the thrust
of a flower

defiant
yet sipping
the liquors
of care

not a question
of do i dare
but when brother
when

the sentences
we all share
mood stanzas
come upon like
crocus in snow

worn heels
over the bed
open hips
like roses
in the rain

the sudden
leap & stop
gestures
frozen
squint the raised
eyes spark

& thrust of
whole body
through
the air
to finger
stillness

THERE
the hawk
of us
all

§

lean growth
the flexed muscles
of sparse earth
spread & quiet

he goes inside
out of the rain
to distill
the flow
into one
thick trickle
one syrup
on a spoon

all that
goes into it
all it
contains
swallowed
& licked
clean

in spite
of his
fears

he don't
give in

§

lone tree
just in the
abstract
words like
rooted
in his
earth

commandeering
the air

all leaf
he lives

no vine

§

caution
tentative
touch

it's air
we share

the ex-
change

of hot
breath

probing
tongue

an un-
easy
embrace

lips
still

we insist
in our
loneliness

§

i walk
like morning
thunder over
the hills

lightning
flashing
from my eyes
i shed

torrents
of rain
i am clean
& wet

in the
morning air
but this
wears at me
makes me
thin a band
closing in

a belt
around
my guts
i can put

it off
but at some
point i must
deal with

the pain
days too
long dreams
too short

what the fuck
i maintain

§

stilled under
a wet blanket
all impulse lost
compass askew all
direction blunted
silence & pain
vector in on
a barren plain

not even
a wildflower
shows its
face